MW00513964

Air Fryer cookbook for Smart people

Cook easy and amazing recipes in a few steps, even if you have no time. Get lean and lose weight with simple and easy recipes

Linda Thompson

© Copyright 2021 - All rights reserved.

The content contained within this book may not be reproduced, duplicated or transmitted without direct written permission from the author or the publisher.

Under no circumstances will any blame or legal responsibility be held against the publisher, or author, for any damages, reparation, or monetary loss due to the information contained within this book. Either directly or indirectly.

Legal Notice:

This book is copyright protected. This book is only for personal use. You cannot amend, distribute, sell, use, quote or paraphrase any part, or the content within this book, without the consent of the author or publisher.

Disclaimer Notice:

Please note the information contained within this document is for educational and entertainment purposes only. All effort has been executed to present accurate, up to date, and reliable, complete information. No warranties of any kind are declared or implied. Readers acknowledge that the author is not engaging in the rendering of legal, financial, medical or professional advice. The content within this book has been derived from various sources. Please consult a licensed professional before attempting any techniques outlined in this book.

By reading this document, the reader agrees that under no circumstances is the author responsible for any losses, direct or indirect, which are incurred as a result of the use of information contained within this document, including, but not limited to, errors, omissions, or inaccuracies.

Table of Contents

Introduction

The Air fryer oven is an easy way to cook delicious healthy meals. It's the perfect appliance for the busy, on-the-go lifestyle. The Air Fryer oven does all the work. In a short amount of time, the Air fryer will showcase a perfectly fried chicken, steak, fish, or wings. The Air fryer oven is also suitable for baking too. You can now bake cakes, pies, and bread that are softer and less greasy when baking.

The Air Fryer has numerous advantages. It's non-stick, BPA-free, easy to clean, and easy to store. See how this Air Fryer does the work for you! It delivers your favorite fried recipes with 65 percent less fat. You can prepare food up to three times faster than in a traditional oven or on the stove. It helps maintain the nutritional content because, in a typical fryer, food is cooked at excessively high temperatures that can destroy nutrients like vitamins and minerals. When your food is prepared in an Air Fryer, it is only cooked to the safe temperatures appropriate for your health and the food. You can prepare healthy meals with less work, more control, and healthier results. It's the most efficient way to cook.

The Air Fryer will substitute these fats with a hot airflow, allowing it to have a crispy and delicious crust. You can control how crispy the crust of your food you want via the controls. You can cook at lower temperatures that are safe for your health, or you can go up to 250 degrees for more crispy goodness. It's easy to cook healthy food with less damage to its nutritional content. It is designed to cook healthier food that tastes better than food cooked in a traditional oil fryer. Cooking healthy food at an exact temperature is easy because every Air Fryer component is perfectly combined. All of your food feels the heat and is cooked evenly.

CHAPTER 1:

Breakfast and Brunch Recipes

1. Veggie Frittata

Preparation Time: 15 minutes

Cooking Time: 25 minutes

Servings: 4

Ingredients:

- ¼ cup chopped red bell pepper

- ¼ cup chopped yellow summer squash

- 2 tbsps. chopped scallion

- 2 tbsps. butter

- Five large eggs, beaten

- ¼ tsp. sea salt

- 1/8 tsp. freshly ground black pepper

- 1 cup shredded Cheddar cheese, divided

Directions:

1. In a 7-inch cake pan, combine the bell pepper, summer squash, and scallion. Add the butter.

2. Set or preheat the air fryer to 350°F. Set the cake pan in the air fryer basket. Cook the vegetables for 3 to 4 minutes or until they are crisp-tender. Remove the pan from the air fryer.

3. Using salt and pepper, beat the eggs in a medium bowl. Stir in half of the Cheddar. Pour into the pan with the vegetables.

4. Return the pan to the air fryer, cook for 10 to 15 minutes, and then top the frittata with the remaining cheese. Cook for another 4 to 5 minutes or until the cheese is melted and the frittata is set. Cut into wedges to serve.

Nutrition:

Calories: 260

Fat: 21g

Cholesterol: 277mg

Carbohydrates: 2g

Fiber: 0g

Protein: 15g

2. Spicy Hash Brown Potatoes

Preparation Time: 15 minutes

Cooking Time: 20 minutes

Servings: 4

Ingredients:

- 2 tbsps. chili powder

- 2 tsp. ground cumin

- 2 tsp. smoked paprika

- 1 tsp. garlic powder

- 1 tsp. cayenne pepper

- 1 tsp. freshly ground black pepper

- Two large russet potatoes, peeled

- 2 tbsps. olive oil

- 1/3 cup chopped onion

- Three garlic cloves, minced

- ½ tsp. sea salt

Directions:

1. For the spice mix: Combine the chili powder, cumin, smoked paprika, garlic powder, cayenne, and black pepper in a small cup. Transfer to a screw-top glass jar and store in a cool, dry

place. (Some of the spice mixes are used in this recipe; save the rest for other uses.)

2. Grate a food processor with the potatoes or on the large holes of a box grater. Put the potatoes in a bowl filled with ice water, and let stand for 10 minutes.

3. When the potatoes have soaked, drain them, and then dry them well with a kitchen towel.

4. Put the olive oil, onion, and garlic in a 7-inch cake pan.

5. Set or preheat the air fryer to 400°F. Put the onion mixture in the air fryer and cook for 3 minutes, and then remove.

6. Put the grated potatoes in a medium bowl and sprinkle with 2 tsp, spice mixture, and toss. Add to the cake pan with the onion mixture.

7. Cook for 10 minutes in an air fryer and then stir the potatoes gently but thoroughly. Cook for 8 to 12 minutes more or until the potatoes are crisp and light golden brown. Season with salt.

Nutrition:

Calories: 235 Fat: 8g

Cholesterol: 0mg Carbohydrates: 39g

Fiber: 5g Protein: 5g

3. Sage and Pear Sausage Patties

Preparation Time: 15 minutes

Cooking Time: 20 minutes

Servings: 6

Ingredients:

- 1pound ground pork

- ¼ cup diced fresh pear

- 1 tbsp. minced fresh sage leaves

- One garlic clove, minced

- ½ tsp. sea salt

- 1/8 tsp. freshly ground black pepper

Directions:

1. In a medium bowl, combine the pork, pear, sage, garlic, salt, and pepper, and mix gently but thoroughly with your hands.

2. Form the mixture into eight equal patties about ½ inches thick.

3. Set or preheat the air fryer to 375°F. Arrange the patties in the air fryer basket in a single layer. In batches, you will have to cook the patties.

4. Cook the sausages for 15 to 20 minutes, flipping them halfway through the cooking time until a meat thermometer registers

160°F. Remove from the air fryer, drain on paper towels for a few minutes, and then serve.

Nutrition:

Calories: 204

Fat: 16g

Cholesterol: 54mg

Carbohydrates: 1g

Fiber: 0g

Protein: 13g

4. Bacon Bombs

Preparation Time: 10 minutes

Cooking Time: 16 minutes

Servings: 4

Ingredients:

- Three center-cut bacon slices

- Three large eggs, lightly beaten

- 1 oz. 1/3-less-fat cream cheese softened

- 1 tbsp. chopped fresh chives

- 4 oz. fresh whole-wheat pizza dough

- Cooking spray

Directions:

1. Sear the bacon slices in a skillet until brown and crispy, then chop into fine crumbles.

2. Add eggs to the same pan and cook for 1 minute, then stir in cream cheese, chives and bacon. Mix well, and then allow this egg filling to cool down. Spread the pizza dough and slice into four -5inches circles.

3. Divide the egg filling on top of each circle and seal its edge to make dumplings. Place the bacon bombs in the Air Fryer basket and spray them with cooking oil.

4. Set the Air Fryer basket inside the Air Fryer toaster oven and close the lid. Select the Air Fry mode at 350 degrees F temperature for 6 minutes. Serve warm.

Nutrition:

Calories: 278

Protein: 7.9g

Carbs: 23g

Fat: 3.9g

5. Morning Potatoes

Preparation Time: 10 minutes **Cooking Time:** 23 minutes

Servings: 4

Ingredients:

- Two russet potatoes, washed & diced ½ tsp. salt

- 1 tbsp. olive oil ¼ tsp. garlic powder

- Chopped parsley for garnish

Directions:

1. Soak the potatoes for 45 minutes in cold water, then drain and dry them.

2. Toss potato cubes with garlic powder, salt, and olive oil in the Air Fryer basket.

3. Set the Air Fryer basket inside the Air Fryer toaster oven and close the lid. Select the Air Fry mode at 400 degrees F temperature for 23 minutes.

4. Toss them well when cooked halfway through, then continue cooking. Garnish with chopped parsley to serve.

Nutrition:

Calories: 146 Protein: 6.2g

Carbs: 41.2g Fat: 5g

6. Breakfast Pockets

Preparation Time: 10 minutes

Cooking Time: 10 minutes

Servings: 6

Ingredients:

- One box puff pastry sheet
- Five eggs
- ½ cup loose sausage, cooked
- ½ cup bacon, cooked
- ½ cup cheddar cheese, shredded

Directions:

1. Cook an egg in a skillet for 1 minute, then mix with sausages, cheddar cheese, and bacon.

2. Spread the pastry sheet and cut it into four rectangles of equal size.

3. Divide the egg mixture over each rectangle. Fold the edges around the filling and seal them.

4. Place the pockets in the Air Fryer basket.

5. Set the Air Fryer basket inside the Air Fryer toaster oven and close the lid. Select the Air Fry mode at 370 degrees F temperature for 10 minutes. Serve warm.

Nutrition:

Calories: 387

Protein: 14.6g

Carbs: 37.4g

Fat: 6g

CHAPTER 2:

Snacks, Appetizers, and Sides

7. Maple Parsnips Mix

Preparation Time: 5 minutes

Cooking Time: 40 minutes

Servings: 6

Ingredients:

- 2 pounds parsnips, roughly cubed

- 2 tbsps. maple syrup

- 1 tbsp. cilantro, chopped

- 1 tbsp. olive oil

Directions:

1. Preheat your air fryer temperature at 360 degrees F, then add the oil and heat it.

2. Add the other ingredients, toss, and cook for 40 minutes.

3. Divide as a side dish between plates and serve.

Nutrition:

Calories 174

Fat 5g

Fiber 3g

Carbs 11g

Protein 4g

8. Air Fried Beets

Preparation Time: 5 minutes

Cooking Time: 35 minutes

Servings: 6

 Ingredients:

- 3 pounds small beets, trimmed and halved

- 4 tbsps. maple syrup

- 1 tbsp. olive oil

Directions:

1. Heat your air fryer at 360 degrees F, then add the oil and heat it.

2. Add the beets and maple syrup, toss, and cook for 35 minutes.

3. Divide the beets between plates and serve as a side dish.

Nutrition:

Calories 171

Fat 4g

Fiber 2g

Carbs 13g

Protein 3g

9. Cauliflower and Chestnuts Risotto

Preparation Time: 10 minutes

Cooking Time: 40 minutes

Servings: 6

Ingredients:

- 2 tbsps. olive oil
- 4 tbsps. soy sauce
- Three garlic cloves, minced
- 1 tbsp. ginger, grated
- Juice of 1 lime
- One cauliflower head, riced
- 10 ounces water chestnuts, drained
- 15 ounces mushrooms, chopped
- One egg whisked

Directions:

1. In your air fryer, mix the cauliflower rice, oil, soy sauce, garlic, ginger, lime juice, chestnuts, and mushrooms.

2. Stir, cover, and cook at 350 degrees F for 20 minutes.

3. Add the egg, toss, and cook at 360 degrees F for 20 minutes more.

4. Divide between plates and serve.

Nutrition:

Calories 182

Fat 3g

Fiber 2g

Carbs 8g

Protein 4g

10. Sumac Eggplants

Preparation Time: 5 minutes

Cooking Time: 20 minutes

Servings: 6

Ingredients:

- 1½ pounds eggplant, cubed

- 1 tbsp. olive oil

- 1 tsp. onion powder

- 1 tsp. sumac

- 2 tsp. za'atar

- Juice of 1 lime

Directions:

1. Place all ingredients in your air fryer and mix well.

2. Cook at 370 degrees F for 20 minutes.

3. Divide as a side dish between plates and serve.

Nutrition:

Calories 182 Fat 4g

Fiber 7g

Carbs 12g

Protein 4g

11. Sesame Cauliflower Mix

Preparation Time: 5 minutes

Cooking Time: 20 minutes

Servings: 4

Ingredients:

- 1 tbsp. olive oil

- One cauliflower head, florets separated

- Three garlic cloves, minced

- Juice of 1 lime

- 1 tbsp. black sesame seeds

Directions:

1. Heat your air fryer at 350 degrees F, then add the oil and heat it.

2. Add the cauliflower, garlic, and lime juice; toss and then cook for 20 minutes.

3. Divide between plates, sprinkle the sesame seeds on top, and serve as a side dish.

Nutrition:

Calories 182 Fat 4g Fiber 3g Carbs 11g

Protein 4 g

12. Salty Rosemary Potatoes

Preparation Time: 10 minutes

Cooking Time: 30 minutes

Servings: 4

Ingredients:

- Four potatoes, thinly sliced

- Salt and black pepper to taste

- 1 tbsp. olive oil

- 2 tsp. rosemary, chopped

Directions:

1. Put all the ingredients in a prepared bowl, mix well, and then transfer to your air fryer's basket.

2. Cook at 370 degrees F for 30 minutes.

3. Divide as a side dish between plates and serve.

Nutrition:

Calories 190

Fat 4g

Fiber 4g

Carbs 14g

Protein 4g

CHAPTER 3:

Vegetable Recipes

13. Vegan Fried Ravioli

Preparation Time: 10 minutes

Cooking Time: 10 minutes

Servings: 4

Ingredients:

- ½ cup of panko breadcrumbs

- 1 tsp. of dried oregano

- Pinch salt & pepper

- 2 tsp. of nutritional yeast flakes

- 1 tsp. of dried basil

- 1 tsp. of garlic powder

- ¼ cup of liquid from a can of chickpeas or other beans*

- 8 oz. of frozen or thawed vegan ravioli**

- Spritz cooking spray

- ½ cup of marinara for dipping

Directions:

1. Mix panko bread. Crumbs, nutritional yeast, garlic powder, flakes, dried basil, dried oregano, pepper, and salt.

2. Put aquafaba into a small separate bowl.

3. Dip ravioli into aquafaba and shake off excess liquid, then dredge in bread crumb mixture.

4. Put ravioli into the air fryer basket. Proceed until all of the ravioli has been breaded.

5. Sprinkle the ravioli with cooking spray.

6. Set Air Fryer to 390 degrees and air fry for 6 minutes. Flip each ravioli over.

7. Get ravioli from Air Fryer and serve with marinara for dipping.

Nutrition:

Calories: 150

Fat: 3g

Carbohydrates: 27 g

Protein: 5g

14. Crispy Veggie Fries

Preparation Time: 10 minutes

Cooking Time: 10 minutes

Servings: 3

Ingredients:

- 2 tbsps. of nutritional yeast flakes, divided

- 1 cup of panko breadcrumbs

- Salt and pepper

- 1 cup of rice flour

- 2 tbsps. of Follow Your Heart Vegan Egg powder*

- 2/3 cup of cold water

- Assorted veggies of choice, cut into bite-size chunks or French fry shapes (such as cauliflower, green beans, sweet onions, zucchini, or squash)

Directions:

1. Set up three dishes on the counter: Place rice flour in one dish and another dish whisk the 2/3 cup water, 1 tbsp. Of the nutritional yeast flakes and Vegan Egg powder. Whisk until smooth.

2. In the last dish, mix 1 tbsp of nutritional yeast, the panko breadcrumbs, and salt and pepper pinches.

3. One veggie fry at a time, dip in the rice flour, followed by Vegan Egg mixture, finally the breadcrumb mixture, pressing gently to set coating. Make as many veggie fries as desired.

4. Lightly spray the Air Fryer basket (or a parchment-lined baking sheet. Place the veggie fries in the basket, give them a quick splash of oil, and set the fryer at 380degreesF for 8 minutes.

Nutrition:

Calories: 134

Fat: 6.6 g

Carbohydrates: 13g

Protein: 1.5 g

Fiber: 20 g

15. Air Fried Carrots, Yellow Squash & Zucchini

Preparation Time: 7 minutes

Cooking Time: 35 minutes

Servings: 4

Ingredients:

- 1 tbsp. Chopped tarragon leaves

- ½tsp. White pepper

- 1 tsp. Salt

- 1pound yellow squash

- 1pound zucchini

- 6 tsp. Olive oil

- ½pound carrots

Directions:

1. Stem and root the end of squash and zucchini and cut in ¾inch half-moons. Peel and cut carrots into 1inch cubes

2. Combine carrot cubes with 2 tsp. Of olive oil, tossing to combine. Pour into air fryer basket and cook 5 minutes at 400 degrees.

3. As carrots cook, drizzle remaining olive oil over squash and zucchini pieces, then season with pepper and salt. Toss well to

coat.

4. Add squash and zucchini when the timer for carrots goes off. Cook for 30 minutes, making sure to toss 23 times during the cooking process.

5. Once done, take out veggies and toss with tarragon. Serve up warm!

Nutrition:

Calories: 122

Fat: 9g

Protein: 6g

Sugar: 0g

16. Cheesy Cauliflower Fritters

Preparation Time: 5 minutes

Cooking Time: 14 minutes

Servings: 8

Ingredients:

- ½c. Chopped parsley

- 1 c. Italian breadcrumbs

- 1 3 c. Shredded mozzarella cheese

- 1 3 c. Shredded sharp cheddar cheese

- One egg

- Two minced garlic cloves

- Three chopped scallions

- One head of cauliflower

Directions:

1. Cut the cauliflower up into florets. Wash well and pat dry. Place into a food processor and pulse 2030 seconds till it looks like rice.

2. Place the cauliflower rice in a bowl and mix with pepper, salt, egg, cheeses, breadcrumbs, garlic, and scallions.

3. With hands, form 15 patties of the mixture. Add more breadcrumbs if needed.

4. With olive oil, spritz patties, and place into your air fryer in a single layer.

5. Cook 14 minutes at 390 degrees, flipping after 7 minutes.

Nutrition:

Calories: 209

Fat: 17g

Protein: 6g

Sugar: 5g

17. Zucchini Parmesan Chips

Preparation Time: 5 minutes

Cooking Time: 8 minutes

Servings: 10

Ingredients:

- ½tsp. Paprika

- ½c. Grated parmesan cheese

- ½c. Italian breadcrumbs

- One lightly beaten egg

- Two thinly sliced zucchinis

Directions:

1. Use a very sharp knife or mandolin slicer to slice zucchini as thinly as you can. Pat off extra moisture.

2. Beat egg with a pinch of pepper and salt and a bit of water.

3. Combine paprika, cheese, and breadcrumbs in a bowl.

4. Dip slices of zucchini into the egg mixture and then into the breadcrumb mixture. Press gently to coat.

5. With olive oil cooking spray, mist coated zucchini slices. Place into your air fryer in a single layer.

6. Cook 8 minutes at 350 degrees.

7. Sprinkle with salt and serve with salsa.

Nutrition:

Calories: 211

Fat: 16g

Protein: 8g

Sugar: 0g

18. Crispy Roasted Broccoli

Preparation Time: 45 minutes

Cooking Time: 10 minutes

Servings: 2

Ingredients:

- ¼tsp. Masala

- ½tsp. Red chili powder

- ½tsp. Salt

- ¼tsp. Turmeric powder

- 1 tbsp. Chickpea flour

- 2 tbsp. Yogurt

- 1pound broccoli

Directions:

1. Cut broccoli up into florets. Soak 2 teaspoons of salt in a bowl of water for at least half an hour to eliminate any impurities.

2. Take out broccoli florets from water and let drain. Wipe down thoroughly.

3. Mix all other ingredients to create a marinade.

4. Toss broccoli florets in the marinade. Cover and chill for 15-30 minutes.

5. Preheat the air fryer to 390 degrees. Place marinated broccoli florets into the fryer. Cook 10 minutes.

6. Five minutes into cooking, shake the basket. Florets will be crispy when done.

Nutrition:

Calories: 96

Fat: 3g

Protein: 7g

Sugar: 5g

19. Crispy Jalapeno Coins

Preparation Time: 10 minutes **Cooking Time:** 8-10 minutes

Servings: 8-10

Ingredients:

- One egg 23 tbsp. Coconut flour

- One sliced and seeded jalapeno

- Pinch of garlic powder Pinch of onion powder

- Pinch of Cajun seasoning (optional)

- Pinch of pepper and salt

Directions:

1. Ensure your air fryer is preheated to 400 degrees.

2. Mix all dry ingredients.

3. Pat jalapeno slices dry. Dip coins into an egg wash and then into the dry mixture. Toss to coat thoroughly.

4. Add coated jalapeno slices to the air fryer in a singular layer. Spray with olive oil.

5. Cook just till crispy.

Nutrition:

Calories: 128 Fat: 8g Protein: 7g

Sugar: 0g

CHAPTER 4:

Poultry Recipes

20. Apricot-Glazed Chicken

Preparation Time: 5 minutes

Cooking Time: 14 minutes

Servings: 2

Ingredients:

- 2 tbsps. apricot preserves

- ½ tsp. minced fresh thyme or 1/8 tsp. dried

- 2 (8-ounce / 227-g) boneless, skinless chicken breasts, trimmed

- 1 tsp. vegetable oil Salt and pepper to taste

Directions:

1. Press Start/Cancel. Preheat the air fryer oven, set the temperature to 400°F (204°C).

2. Microwave apricot preserves and thyme in the bowl until fluid, about 30 seconds; set aside. Pound chicken to uniform thickness as needed. Pat dry using paper towels, rub with oil, and season with salt and pepper.

3. Arrange breasts skin-side down in a fry basket, spaced evenly apart, alternating ends. Insert the fry basket at mid position. Select Air Fry, Convection, and set time to 4 minutes. Flip chicken and brush skin side with the apricot-thyme mixture. Air fry until chicken registers 160°F (71°C), 10 minutes more.

4. Take the chicken to a serving platter, tent loosely with aluminum foil, and let rest for 5 minutes. Serve.

Nutrition:

Energy (calories): 62 kcal

Protein: 0.56 g

Fat: 2.36 g

Carbohydrates: 10.87 g

21. Parmesan Chicken Wings

Preparation Time: 15 minutes

Cooking Time: 17 minutes

Servings: 4

Ingredients:

- 1¼ cups grated Parmesan cheese

- 1 tbsp. garlic powder

- 1 tsp. salt

- ½ tsp. freshly ground black pepper

- ¾ cup all-purpose flour

- One large egg, beaten

- 12 chicken wings (about 1 pound / 454 g)

- Cooking spray

Directions:

1. Press Start/Cancel. Preheat the air fryer oven to 390°F (199°C). Line the fry basket with parchment paper.

2. In a shallow bowl, whisk the Parmesan cheese, garlic powder, salt, and pepper until blended. Place the flour in a second shallow bowl and the beaten egg in a third shallow bowl.

3. One at a time, dip the chicken wings into the flour, the beaten egg, and the Parmesan cheese mixture, coating thoroughly.

4. Place the chicken wings on the parchment and spritz with cooking spray. Insert the fry basket at mid position.

5. Select Air Fry, Convection, and set time to 8 minutes. Flip the chicken, spritz it with cooking spray, and air fry for 9 minutes more until the internal temperature reaches 165°F (74°C) and the insides are no longer pink. Let sit for 5 minutes before serving.

Nutrition:

Energy (calories): 348 kcal

Protein: 31.49 g

Fat: 13.16 g

Carbohydrates: 24.16 g

22. Herb-Buttermilk Chicken Breast

Preparation Time: 5 minutes

Cooking Time: 43 minutes

Servings: 2

Ingredients:

- One large bone-in, skin-on chicken breast
- 1 cup buttermilk 1½ tsp. dried parsley
- 1½ tsp. dried chives ¾ tsp. kosher salt
- ½ tsp. dried dill ½ tsp. onion powder
- ¼ tsp. garlic powder ¼ tsp. dried tarragon
- Cooking spray

Directions:

1. Place the chicken breast in a bowl and pour over the buttermilk, turning the chicken in it to make sure it's completely covered. Let the chicken stand at room temperature for at least 20 minutes or in the refrigerator for up to 4 hours.

2. Meanwhile, in a bowl, stir together the parsley, chives, salt, dill, onion powder, garlic powder, and tarragon.

3. Press Start/Cancel. Preheat the air fryer oven to 300°F (149°C).

4. Grab the chicken from the buttermilk, letting the excess drip off, and then place the chicken skin-side up directly in the food tray. Sprinkle the seasoning mix all over the top of the chicken breast, then let stand until the herb mix soaks into the buttermilk, at least 5 minutes.

5. Spray the top of the chicken using the cooking spray. Insert the food tray at a low position. Select Bake, Convection, and set time to 10 minutes. Then increase the temperature to 350°F (177°C) and bake until an instant-read thermometer inserted into the thickest part of the breast reads 160°F (71°C), and the chicken is deep golden brown, 33 minutes.

6. Move the chicken breast place to a cutting board, let rest for 10 minutes, then cut the meat off the bone and cut into thick slices for serving.

Nutrition:

Energy (calories): 55 kcal Protein: 4.35 g

Fat: 1.19 g

Carbohydrates: 7.08 g

23. Nutty Chicken Tenders

Preparation Time: 5 minutes

Cooking Time: 12 minutes

Servings: 4

Ingredients:

- 1 pound (454 g) chicken tenders

- 1 tsp. kosher salt

- 1 tsp. black pepper

- ½ tsp. smoked paprika

- ¼ cup coarse mustard

- 2tbsps. honey

- 1 cup finely crushed pecans

Directions:

1. Press Start/Cancel. Preheat the air fryer oven, set the temperature to 350°F (177°C).

2. Place the chicken in a large bowl. Sprinkle with salt, pepper, and paprika. Toss until the spices are mixed with the chicken. Add the mustard and honey and toss until the chicken is coated.

3. Place the pecans on a plate. Roll the chicken into the pecans until both sides are coated, dealing with one piece of chicken at a time. Lightly brush off any loose pecans. Place the chicken in the fry basket. Insert at a low position.

4. Select Bake, Convection, and set time to 12 minutes or until the chicken be cooked through and the pecans are golden brown.

5. Serve warm.

Nutrition:

Energy (calories): 501 kcal

Protein: 21.54 g

Fat: 33.01 g

Carbohydrates: 33.53 g

24. Paprika Indian Fennel Chicken

Preparation Time: 10 minutes

Cooking Time: 15 minutes

Servings: 4

Ingredients:

- 1 pound or (454 g) boneless, skinless chicken thighs, cut crosswise into thirds
- One yellow onion, cut into 1½-inch-thick slices
- 1 tbsp. coconut oil, melted 2 tsp. minced fresh ginger
- 2 tsp. minced garlic 1 tsp. smoked paprika
- 1 tsp. ground fennel 1 tsp. garam masala
- 1 tsp. ground turmeric
- 1 tsp. kosher salt
- ½ to 1 tsp. cayenne pepper
- Vegetable oil spray
- 2 tsp. fresh lemon juice
- ¼ cup chopped fresh cilantro or parsley

Directions:

1. Use a fork to make a hole in the chicken all over to enable greater penetration of the marinade.

2. In a large bowl, combine the onion, coconut oil, ginger, garlic, paprika, fennel, garam masala, turmeric, salt, and cayenne. Add the chicken, toss to combine, marinate at room temperature for 30 minutes, or cover and refrigerate for up to 24 hours.

3. Press Start/Cancel. Preheat the air fryer oven, set the temperature to 350°F (177°C).

4. Place the chicken and onion in the fry basket. (Discard remaining marinade.) Spray with some vegetable oil spray. Insert the fry basket at mid position.

5. Select Air Fry, Convection, and set time to 15 minutes. Halfway through the cooking time, remove the basket, spray the chicken and onion with more vegetable oil spray, and toss gently to coat. Using a meat thermometer at the end of cooking time to ensure that the chicken has reached an internal temperature of 165F (74C).

6. Transfer the chicken and onion to a serving platter. Sprinkle with lemon juice and cilantro and serve.

Nutrition:

Energy (calories): 237 kcal Protein: 10.98 g

Fat: 10.08 g Carbohydrates: 25.82 g

25. Crispy Chicken Cordon Bleu

Preparation Time: 15 minutes

Cooking Time: 14 minutes

Servings: 4

Ingredients:

- 14 chicken breast fillets

- ¼ cup chopped ham

- $1/3$ cup grated Swiss or Gruyère cheese

- ¼ cup flour

- Pinch salt

- Freshly ground black pepper to taste

- ½ tsp. dried marjoram

- One egg

- 1 cup panko bread crumbs

- Olive oil for misting

Directions:

1. Press Start/Cancel. Preheat the air fryer oven to 380°F (193°C).

2. Put the chicken breast fillets on a work surface and gently press them with the palm of your hand to make them a bit

thinner. Don't tear the meat.

3. In a small bowl, combine the ham and cheese. Divide this mixture among the chicken fillets. Wrap the chicken around the filling to enclose it, using toothpicks to hold the chicken together.

4. In a prepared shallow bowl, mix the flour, salt, pepper, and marjoram. In another bowl, beat the egg. Spread the bread crumbs out on a plate.

5. Dip the chicken into the flour mixture, then into the egg, then into the bread crumbs to coat thoroughly.

6. Put the chicken in the fry basket and mist with olive oil. Insert at a low position.

7. Select Bake, Convection, and set time to 14 minutes, or until the chicken is thoroughly cooked to 165°F (74°C). Carefully remove the toothpicks and serve.

Nutrition:

Energy (calories): 189 kcal

Protein: 10.94 g

Fat: 9.74 g

Carbohydrates: 14.07 g

26. Thai Curry Meatballs

Preparation Time: 10 minutes

Cooking Time: 10 minutes

Servings: 4

Ingredients:

- 1 pound (454 g) ground chicken

- ¼ cup chopped fresh cilantro

- 1 tsp. chopped fresh mint

- 1 tbsp. fresh lime juice

- 1 tbsp. Thai red, green, or yellow curry paste

- 1 tbsp. fish sauce

- Two garlic cloves, minced

- 2 tsp. minced fresh ginger

- ½ tsp. kosher salt

- ½ tsp. black pepper

- ¼ tsp. red pepper flakes

Directions:

1. Press Start/Cancel. Preheat the air fryer oven, set the temperature to 400°F (204°C).

2. In a prepared large bowl, gently mix the ground chicken, cilantro, mint, lime juice, curry paste, fish sauce, garlic, ginger, salt, black pepper, and red pepper flakes until thoroughly combined.

3. Form the mixture into 16 meatballs. Place the meatballs in a single layer in the fry basket. Insert the fry basket at mid position. Select Air Fry, Convection, and set time to 10 minutes, turning the meatballs halfway through the cooking time. To ensure that the meatballs have reached a 165F (74C) internal temperature, use a meat thermometer. Serve immediately.

Nutrition:

Energy (calories): 257 kcal

Protein: 30.53 g

Fat: 13.79 g

Carbohydrates: 2.62 g

CHAPTER 5:

Beef Recipes

27. Warming Winter Beef with Celery

Preparation Time: 5 minutes

Cooking Time: 12 minutes

Servings: 4

Ingredients

- 9 ounces tender beef, chopped

- 1/2 cup leeks, chopped

- 1/2 cup celery stalks, chopped

- Two cloves of garlic smashed

- 2 tbsps. red cooking wine

- 3/4 cup cream of celery soup

- Two sprigs of rosemary, chopped

- 1/4 tsp. smoked paprika

- 3/4 tsp. salt

- 1/4 tsp. black pepper, or to taste

Directions:

1. Add the beef, leeks, celery, and garlic to the baking dish; cook

   for about 5 minutes at 390 degrees F.

2. Once the meat is starting to tender, pour in the wine and soup.

   Season with rosemary, smoked paprika, salt, and black pepper.

   Now, cook an additional 7 minutes.

Nutrition:

Calories: 103 kcal

Protein: 14.2 g

Fat: 3.4 g

Carbohydrates: 4.07 g

28. Beef & Veggie Spring Rolls

Preparation Time: 5 minutes

Cooking Time: 12 minutes

Servings: 10

Ingredients

- 2-ounce Asian rice noodles

- 1 tbsp. sesame oil

- 7-ounce ground beef

- One small onion, chopped

- Three garlic cloves, crushed

- 1 cup fresh mixed vegetables

- 1 tsp. soy sauce

- One packet spring roll skins

- 2 tbsps. water

- Olive oil, as required

Directions:

1. Soak the noodles in warm water till soft.

2. Drain and cut into small lengths. In a pan, heat the oil and add the onion and garlic and sauté for about 4-5 minutes.

3. Add beef and cook for about 4-5 minutes.

4. Add vegetables and cook for about 5-7 minutes or till cooked through.

5. Stir in soy sauce and remove from the heat.

6. Immediately, stir in the noodles and keep aside till all the juices have been absorbed.

7. Preheat the Air Fryer Oven to 350 degrees F.

8. Place the spring rolls skin onto a smooth surface.

9. Add a line of the filling diagonally across.

10. Fold the top point over the filling and then fold in both sides.

11. On the final point, brush it with water before rolling to seal.

12. Brush the spring rolls with oil.

13. Arrange the rolls in batches in the air fryer and Cook for about 8 minutes.

14. Repeat with remaining rolls. Now, place spring rolls onto a baking sheet.

15. Bake for about 6 minutes per side.

Nutrition:

Energy (calories): 289 kcal Protein: 3.54 g

Fat: 29.39 g

Carbohydrates: 4.55 g

29. Charred Onions And Steak Cube BBQ

Preparation Time: 5 minutes

Cooking Time: 40 minutes

Servings: 3

Ingredients

- 1 cup red onions, cut into wedges

- 1 tbsp. dry mustard

- 1 tbsp. olive oil

- 1-pound boneless beef sirloin, cut into cubes

- Salt and pepper to taste

Directions:

1. Preheat the air fryer to 390°F.

2. Place the grill pan accessory in the air fryer.

3. Toss all ingredients in a bowl and mix until everything is coated with the seasonings.

4. Place on the grill pan and cook for 40 minutes.

5. Halfway through the cooking time, give a stir to cook evenly.

Nutrition:

Calories: 260 Fat: 10.7g Protein: 35.5g

30. Beef Stroganoff

Preparation Time: 10 minutes

Cooking Time: 14 minutes

Servings: 4

Ingredients

- 9 Oz's Tender Beef

- 1 Onion, chopped

- 1 Tbsp. Paprika

- 3/4 Cup Sour Cream

- Salt and Pepper to taste

- Baking Dish

Directions:

1. Preheat the Air Fryer Oven to 390 degrees.

2. Chop the beef and marinate it using paprika.

3. Add the chopped onions into the baking dish and heat for about 2 minutes in the Air Fryer Oven.

4. Add the beef into the dish when the onions are transparent, and cook for 5 minutes.

5. Once the beef is starting to tender, pour in the sour cream and cook for another 7 minutes.

6. At this point, the liquid should have reduced. Season with salt and pepper and serve.

Nutrition:

Energy (calories): 79 kcal

Protein: 2.28 g

Fat: 4.84 g

Carbohydrates: 7.61 g

31. Cheesy Ground Beef And Mac Taco Casserole

Preparation Time: 10 minutes

Cooking Time: 25 minutes

Servings: 5

Ingredients

- 1-ounce shredded Cheddar cheese

- 1-ounce shredded Monterey Jack cheese

- 2 tbsps. chopped green onions

- 1/2 (10.75 ounces) can condensed tomato soup

- 1/2-pound lean ground beef

- 1/2 cup crushed tortilla chips

- 1/4-pound macaroni, cooked according to manufacturer's Instructions

- 1/4 cup chopped onion

- 1/4 cup sour cream (optional)

- 1/2 (1.25 ounce) package taco seasoning mix

- 1/2 (14.5 ounces) can diced tomatoes

Directions:

1. Lightly grease the baking pan of the air fryer with cooking spray. Add onion and ground beef. For 10 minutes, cook on

360°F. Halfway through cooking time, stir and crumble ground beef.

2. Add taco seasoning, diced tomatoes, and tomato soup. Mix well. Mix in pasta.

3. Sprinkle crushed tortilla chips. Sprinkle cheese.

4. Cook for 15 minutes at 390°F until tops are lightly browned and cheese is melted.

5. Serve and enjoy.

Nutrition:

Calories: 329

Fat: 17g

Protein: 15.6g

32. Beefy Steak Topped with Chimichurri Sauce

Preparation Time: 5 minutes

Cooking Time: 60 minutes

Servings: 6

Ingredients

- 1 cup commercial chimichurri

- 3 pounds steak

- Salt and pepper to taste

Directions:

1. Place all ingredients in a Ziploc bag and marinate in the fridge for 2 hours.

2. Preheat the air fryer to 390°F.

3. Place the grill pan accessory in the air fryer.

4. Grill the skirt steak for 20 minutes per batch.

5. Flip the steak every 10 minutes for even grilling.

Nutrition:

Calories: 50

Fat: 27g

Protein: 63 g

CHAPTER 6:

Pork and Lamb Recipes

33. Mint Lamb with Roasted Hazelnuts

Preparation Time: 10 minutes

Cooking Time: 25 minutes

Servings: 2

Ingredients

- ¼ cup hazelnuts, toasted

- 2/3 lb. shoulder of lamb cut into strips

- 1 tbsp. hazelnut oil

- 1 tbsp. fresh mint leaves chopped

- ½ cup frozen peas

- ¼ cup of water

- ½ cup white wine

- Salt and black pepper to taste

Directions:

1. Toss lamb with hazelnuts, spices, and all the ingredients in a baking pan.

2. Press the "Power Button" of the Air Fry Oven and turn the dial to select the "Bake" mode.

3. Press the Time button and again turn the dial to set the cooking time to 25 minutes.

4. Now push the Temp button and rotate the dial to set the temperature at 370 degrees F.

5. When preheated, put the baking pan in the oven and close its lid.

6. Slice and serve warm.

Nutrition:

Calories 322

Fat 11.8 g

Cholesterol 56 mg

Carbs 14.6 g

Fiber 4.4 g

Protein 19.3 g

34. Lamb Rack with Lemon Crust

Preparation Time: 10 minutes

Cooking Time: 25 minutes

Servings: 5

Ingredients

- 1.7 lbs. frenched rack of lamb

- Salt and black pepper to taste

- 0.13-lb. dry breadcrumbs

- 1 tsp. grated garlic

- 1/2 tsp. salt

- 1 tsp. cumin seeds

- 1 tsp. ground cumin

- 1 tsp. oil

- ½ tsp. Grated lemon rind

- One egg, beaten

Directions:

1. Place the lamb rack in a baking tray and pour the whisked egg on top.

2. Whisk the rest of the crusting ingredients in a bowl and spread over the lamb.

3. Press the "Power Button" of the Air Fry Oven and turn the dial to select the "Air Fry" mode.

4. Press the Time button and again turn the dial to set the cooking time to 25 minutes.

5. Now push the Temp button and rotate the dial to set the temperature at 350 degrees F.

6. Once preheated, place the lamb baking tray in the oven and close its lid.

7. Slice and serve warm.

Nutrition:

Calories 427

Fat 5.4 g

Cholesterol 168 mg

Sodium 203 mg

Carbs 58.5 g

Fiber 4 g

Protein 21.9 g

35. Braised Lamb Shanks

Preparation Time: 10 minutes

Cooking Time: 10 minutes

Servings: 4

Ingredients

- Four lamb shanks

- 1½ tsp. salt

- ½ tsp. black pepper

- Four garlic cloves, crushed

- 2 tbsps. olive oil

- 4 to 6 sprigs of fresh rosemary

- 3 cups beef broth, divided

- 2 tbsps. balsamic vinegar

Directions:

1. Place the sham shanks in a baking pan.

2. Whisk the rest of the ingredients in a bowl and pour over the shanks.

3. Place these shanks in the Air fryer basket.

4. Press the "Power Button" of the Air Fry Oven and turn the dial to select the "Air Fry" mode.

5. Press the Time button and again turn the dial to set the cooking time to 20 minutes.

6. Now push the Temp button and rotate the dial to set the temperature at 360 degrees F.

7. Once preheated, place the Air fryer basket in the oven and close its lid.

8. Slice and serve warm.

Nutrition:

Calories 336

Fat 9.7 g

Cholesterol 181 mg

Carbs 32.5 g

Fiber 0.3 g

Sugar 1.8 g

Protein 30.3 g

36. Za'atar Lamb Chops

Preparation Time: 10 minutes

Cooking Time: 10 minutes

Servings: 8

Ingredients

- 8 lamb loin chops, bone-in

- 4 garlic cloves, crushed

- 1 tsp. olive oil

- 1/2 fresh lemon

- 1 1/4 tsp. salt

- 1 tbsp. Za'atar

- Black pepper to taste

Directions:

1. Rub the lamb chops with oil, za'atar, salt, lemon juice, garlic, and black pepper.

2. Place these chops in the air fryer basket.

3. Press the "Power Button" of the Air Fry Oven and turn the dial to select the "Air Fry" mode.

4. Press the Time button and again turn the dial to set the cooking time to 10 minutes.

5. Now push the Temp button and rotate the dial to set the temperature at 400 degrees F.

6. Once preheated, place the air fryer basket in the oven and close its lid.

7. Flip the chops when cooked halfway through, then resume cooking.

8. Serve warm.

Nutrition:

Calories 391

Fat 2.8 g

Cholesterol 330 mg

Carbs 36.5 g

Fiber 9.2 g

Protein 6.6

37. Lamb Sirloin Steak

Preparation Time: 10 minutes

Cooking Time: 15 minutes

Servings: 2

Ingredients

- 1/2 onion

- Four slices ginger

- Five cloves garlic

- 1 tsp. garam masala

- 1 tsp. fennel, ground

- 1 tsp. cinnamon ground

- 1/2 tsp. cardamom ground

- 1 tsp. cayenne

- 1 tsp. salt

- 1-lb. boneless lamb sirloin steaks

Directions:

1. In a blender, jug adds all the ingredients except the chops.

2. Rub the chops with this blended mixture and marinate for 30 minutes.

3. Transfer the chops to the Air fryer basket.

4. Press the "Power Button" of the Air Fry Oven and turn the dial to select the "Air Fry" mode.

5. Press the Time button and again turn the dial to set the cooking time to 15 minutes.

6. Now push the Temp button and rotate the dial to set the temperature at 330 degrees F.

7. Once preheated, place the Air fryer basket in the oven and close its lid.

8. Flip the chops when cooked halfway through, then resume cooking.

9. Serve warm.

Nutrition:

Calories 453

Fat 2.4 g

Cholesterol 21 mg

Carbs 18 g

Fiber 2.3 g

Protein 23.2 g

CHAPTER 7:

Fish and Seafood Recipes

38. Shrimp with Garlic Sauce

Preparation Time: 10 minutes

Cooking Time: 13 minutes

Servings: 4

Ingredients

- 1 1/4 lbs. shrimp, peeled and deveined

- 1/4 cup butter

- 1 tbsp. minced garlic

- 2 tbsp. fresh lemon juice

- Salt and pepper 1/8 tsp. Red pepper flakes

- 2 tbsp. minced fresh parsley

Directions:

1. Toss the shrimp with oil and all other ingredients in a bowl.

2. Spread the seasoned shrimp in the baking pan.

3. Press the "Power Button" of the Air Fry Oven and turn the dial to select the "Bake" mode.

4. Press the Time button and again turn the dial to set the cooking time to 13 minutes.

5. Now push the Temp button and rotate the dial to set the temperature at 350 degrees F.

6. When preheated, place the baking pan in the oven and close its lid.

7. Serve warm.

Nutrition:

Calories 207

Fat 14.1g

Cholesterol 212mg

Carbohydrate 2.3g

Fiber 0.1g

Protein 19.1g

39. Shrimp Scampi

Preparation Time: 10 minutes

Cooking Time: 13 minutes

Servings: 8

Ingredients

- 2 lbs. jumbo shrimp, deveined and peeled

- 3 tbsps. olive oil

- 4 tbsps. lemon juice

- 2 tsp. salt

- 1/2 tsp. black pepper

- 1/4 cup butter

- Four cloves garlic, minced

- One small shallot, minced

- 2 tbsps. minced fresh parsley

- 1/2 tsp. dried oregano

- 1/4 tsp. crushed red pepper flakes

- One egg yolk 2/3 cup panko bread crumbs

Directions:

1. Toss shrimp with egg, spices, seasonings, oil, herbs, butter, and

   shallots in a bowl.

2. Mix well, and then add breadcrumbs to coat well.

3. Spread the shrimp in a baking tray in a single layer.

4. Press the "Power Button" of the Air Fry Oven and turn the dial to select the "Bake" mode.

5. Press the Time button and again turn the dial to set the cooking time to 13 minutes.

6. Now push the Temp button and rotate the dial to set the temperature at 425 degrees F.

7. Once preheated, place the shrimp's baking tray in the oven and close its lid.

8. Toss and flip the shrimp when cooked halfway through.

9. Serve warm.

Nutrition:

Calories 220

Fat 13.2g

Cholesterol 181mg

Carbohydrate 8.2g

Fiber 0.5g

Protein 16.8g

40. Shrimp Parmesan Bake

Preparation Time: 10 minutes

Cooking Time: 8 minutes

Servings: 4

Ingredients

- 1 1/2 lb. large raw shrimp, peeled and deveined

- 1/4 cup melted butter

- 1 tsp. coarse salt

- 1/4 tsp. black pepper

- 1 tsp. garlic powder

- 1/2 tsp. crushed red pepper

- 1/4 cup Parmesan cheese, grated

Directions:

1. Toss the shrimp with oil and all other ingredients in a bowl.

2. Spread the seasoned shrimp in the Baking tray.

3. Press the "Power Button" of the Air Fry Oven and turn the dial to select the "Bake" mode.

4. Press the Time button and again turn the dial to set the cooking time to 8 minutes.

5. Now push the Temp button and rotate the dial to set the temperature at 400 degrees F.

6. Once preheated, place the lobster's baking tray in the oven and close its lid.

7. Switch the Air fryer oven to broil mode and cook for 1 minute.

8. Serve warm.

Nutrition:

Calories 231

Fat 14.9g

Cholesterol 249mg

Carbohydrate 2.3g

Fiber 0.2g

Protein 23.3g

41. Shrimp in Lemon Sauce

Preparation Time: 10 minutes

Cooking Time: 8 minutes

Servings: 4

Ingredients

- 1 1/4 lbs. large shrimp, peeled and deveined

- Cooking spray

- 1/4 cup fresh lemon juice

- 2 tbsps. light butter, melted

- Three garlic cloves, minced

- 1 tsp. Worcestershire sauce

- 3/4 tsp. lemon-pepper seasoning

- 1/4 tsp. ground red pepper

- 2 tbsps. chopped fresh parsley

Directions;

1. Toss the shrimp with oil and all other ingredients in a bowl.

2. Spread the seasoned shrimp in the baking tray.

3. Press the "Power Button" of the Air Fry Oven and turn the dial to select the "Air Roast" mode.

4. Press the Time button and again turn the dial to set the cooking time to 8 minutes.

5. Now push the Temp button and rotate the dial to set the temperature at 425 degrees F.

6. Once preheated, place the shrimp's baking tray in the oven and close its lid.

7. Serve warm.

Nutrition:

Calories 176

Fat 6.1g

Cholesterol 218mg

Sodium 237mg

Carbohydrate 4.3g

Fiber 0.3g

Protein 27g

42. Bacon-Wrapped Shrimp

Preparation Time: 5 minutes

Cooking Time: 5 minutes

Servings: 4

Ingredients

- 1¼ pound tiger shrimp, peeled and deveined

- 1 pound bacon

Directions:

1. Preparing the **Ingredients:** Wrap each shrimp with a slice of bacon. Refrigerate for about 20 minutes. Preheat the Air fryer oven to 390 degrees F.

2. Air Frying: Arrange the shrimp in the Oven rack/basket. Place the rack in the middle of the Air Fryer Oven shelf. Cook for about 5-7 minutes.

Nutrition:

Energy (calories): 493 kcal

Protein: 41.06 g

Fat: 35.4 g

Carbohydrates: 7.17 g

43. Quick Paella

Preparation Time: 7 minutes

Cooking Time: 15 minutes

Servings: 4

Ingredients

- 1 (10-ounce) package frozen cooked rice, thawed

- 1 (6-ounce) jar artichoke hearts, drained and chopped

- ¼ cup vegetable broth

- ½ tsp. turmeric

- ½ tsp. dried thyme

- 1 cup frozen cooked small shrimp

- ½ cup frozen baby peas

- One tomato, diced

Directions:

1. Preparing the **Ingredients**. In a 6-by-6-by-2-inch pan, combine the rice, artichoke hearts, vegetable broth, turmeric, and thyme, and stir gently.

2. Air Frying. Place in the Air fryer oven. Set temperature to 360°F, and bake for 8 to 9 minutes or until the rice is hot. Remove from the air fryer and gently stir in the shrimp, peas,

and tomato. Cook for 5 to 8 minutes or until the shrimp and peas are hot and the paella is bubbling.

Nutrition:

Calories: 345

Fat: 1

Protein: 18g

Fiber: 4g

44. Coconut Shrimp

Preparation Time: 15 minutes

Cooking Time: 5 minutes

Servings: 4

Ingredients

- 1 (8-ounce) can crushed pineapple
- ½ cup sour cream
- ¼ cup pineapple preserves
- egg whites
- 2/3 cup cornstarch
- 2/3 cup sweetened coconut
- 1 cup panko bread crumbs
- 1 pound uncooked large shrimp, thawed if frozen, deveined and shelled
- Olive oil for misting

Directions:

1. Preparing the **Ingredients**. Drain the crushed pineapple well, then reserve the juice. In a small bowl, combine the pineapple, sour cream, and preserves, and mix well. Just set aside. In a prepared shallow bowl, beat the egg whites with 2 tbsps. of the

reserved pineapple liquid. On a plate, put the cornstarch. On another plate, combine the coconut and bread crumbs. Immerse the shrimp into the cornstarch, shake it off, then dip it into the mixture of white eggs and then into the mixture of coconuts. Place the shrimp in the air fryer rack/basket and mist with oil.

2. Air Frying. Set temperature to 360°F. Air-fry for 5 to 7 minutes or until the shrimp are crisp and golden brown.

Nutrition:

Calories: 524

Fat: 14g

Protein: 33g

Fiber: 4g

CHAPTER 8:

Bakery and Desserts

45. Plum Bars

Preparation Time: 10 minutes

Cooking Time: 16 minutes

Servings: 8

Ingredients:

- 2 cups dried plums

- 6 tbsps. water

- 2 cup rolled oats

- 1 cup brown sugar

- ½ tsp. baking soda

- 1 tsp. cinnamon powder

- 2 tbsps. butter, melted

- 1 egg, whisked

- Cooking spray

Directions:

1. In your food processor, mix plums with water and blend until you obtain a sticky spread.

2. In a bowl, mix oats with cinnamon, baking soda, sugar, egg, and butter and whisk really well.

3. Press half of the oats mix in a baking pan that fits your air fryer sprayed with cooking oil, spread plums mix, and top with the other half of the oats mix.

4. Introduce in your air fryer and cook at 350 degrees F for 16 minutes.

5. Leave mix aside to cool down, cut into medium bars, and serve.

6. Enjoy!

Nutrition:

Calories 111

Fat 5g

Fiber 6g

Carbs 12g

Protein 6 g

46. Plum and Currant Tart

Preparation Time: 30 minutes

Cooking Time: 35 minutes

Servings: 6

Ingredients:

For the crumble:

- ¼ cup almond flour

- ¼ cup millet flour

- 1 cup brown rice flour

- ½ cup cane sugar

- 10 tbsps. butter, soft

- 3 tbsps. milk

For the filling:

- 1 pound small plums, pitted and halved

- 1 cup white currants

- 2 tbsps. cornstarch

- 3 tbsps. sugar

- ½ tsp. vanilla extract

- ½ tsp. cinnamon powder

- ¼ tsp. ginger powder

- 1 tsp. lime juice

Directions:

1. In a bowl, mix brown rice flour with ½ cup sugar, millet flour, almond flour, butter, and milk and stir until you obtain sand-like dough.

2. Reserve ¼ of the dough, press the rest of the dough into a tart pan that fits your air fryer and keep in the fridge for 30 minutes.

3. Meanwhile, in a bowl, mix plums with currants, 3 tbsps. sugar, cornstarch, vanilla extract, cinnamon, ginger, and lime juice and stir well.

4. Pour this over tart crust, crumble reserved dough on top, introduce in your air fryer and cook at 350 degrees F for 35 minutes.

5. Leave the tart to cool down, slice, and serve.

6. Enjoy!

Nutrition:

Calories 200 Fat 5g

Fiber 4g Carbs 8g

Protein 6g

47. Cashew Bars

Preparation Time: 10 minutes

Cooking Time: 15 minutes

Servings: 6

Ingredients:

- 1/3 cup honey

- ¼ cup almond meal

- 1 tbsp. almond butter

- 1 and ½ cups cashews, chopped

- 4 dates, chopped

- ¾ cup coconut, shredded

- 1 tbsp. chia seeds

Directions:

1. In a bowl, mix honey with almond meal and almond butter and stir well.

2. Add cashews, coconut, dates, and chia seeds and stir well again.

3. Spread this on a lined baking sheet that fits your air fryer and press well.

4. Introduce in the fryer and cook at 300 degrees F for 15 minutes.

5. Leave the mix to cool down, cut into medium bars and serve.

6. Enjoy!

Nutrition:

Calories 121

Fat 4g

Fiber 7g

Carbs 5g

Protein 6 g

48. Brown Butter Cookies

Preparation Time: 10 minutes

Cooking Time: 10 minutes

Servings: 6

Ingredients:

- 1 and ½ cups butter

- 2 cups brown sugar

- 2 eggs, whisked

- 3 cups flour

- 2/3 cup pecans, chopped

- 2 tsp. vanilla extract

- 1 tsp. baking soda

- ½ tsp. baking powder

Directions:

1. Heat a pan with the butter over medium heat, stir until it melts, add brown sugar and stir until this dissolves.

2. In a bowl, mix flour with pecans, vanilla extract, baking soda, baking powder, and eggs and stir well.

3. Add brown butter, stir well and arrange spoonfuls of this mix on a lined baking sheet that fits your air fryer.

4. Introduce in the fryer and cook at 340 degrees F for 10 minutes.

5. Leave cookies to cool down and serve.

6. Enjoy!

Nutrition:

Calories 144

Fat 5g

Fiber 6g

Carbs 19 g

Protein 2g

49. Sweet Potato Cheesecake

Preparation Time: 10 minutes

Cooking Time: 5 minutes

Servings: 4

Ingredients:

- 4 tbsps. butter, melted

- 6 ounces mascarpone, soft

- 8 ounces cream cheese, soft

- 2/3 cup graham crackers, crumbled

- ¾ cup milk

- 1 tsp. vanilla extract

- 2/3 cup sweet potato puree

- ¼ tsp. cinnamon powder

Directions:

1. In a bowl, mix butter with crumbled crackers, stir well, press on the bottom of a cake pan that fits your air fryer and keep in the fridge for now.

2. In another bowl, mix cream cheese with mascarpone, sweet potato puree, milk, cinnamon, and vanilla and whisk really well.

3. Spread this over crust, introduce in your air fryer, cook at 300 degrees F for 4 minutes and keep in the fridge for a few hours before serving.

4. Enjoy!

Nutrition:

Calories 172

Fat 4g

Fiber 6 g

Carbs 8g

Protein 3g

50. Air-Fried Plantains

Preparation Time: 10 minutes

Cooking Time: 20 minutes

Servings: 4

Ingredients:

- Avocado or sunflower oil (2 tsp.)

- Ripened/almost brown – plantains (2)

- Optional: Salt (.125 tsp.)

Directions:

1. Warm up the Air Fryer to 400° Fahrenheit.

2. Slice the plantains at an angle for a .5-inch thickness.

3. Mix the oil, salt, and plantains in a container, coat the surface thoroughly.

4. Set the timer for eight to ten minutes; shake after five minutes. Add a minute or two more to your desired doneness.

Nutrition:

Calories 130

Fat 3 g

Protein 1 g

Conclusion

I hope this Air Fryer Toaster Oven Cookbook allows you to understand this groundbreaking kitchen appliance's dynamics and principles, why you should use it, and how it's going to change your outlook on food preparation, creative cooking, and healthier lifestyles. The Air fryer Toaster Oven has all the benefits of a toaster oven, with the powerful air frying technology of an air fryer. The air fryer toaster oven will make you forget your old toaster oven. The controls are easy, intuitive and on display, like the air fryer. You don't need to worry about a frying pan clean-up either. The heavy "chicken" bottom cavity of the toaster oven can also get hot enough to cook your food in a short amount of time. An air fryer is the perfect kitchen appliance for toaster oven people. Now you can cook your bread, pizza, chicken, meat and fish, store in air fryer toaster oven without oils for long-lasting taste.

I encourage you to share these recipes with family and friends, tell them about this cookbook, and let them know about Air fryer toaster oven's benefits. This cookbook will prepare you to obtain the ultimate in performance and convenience by taking full advantage of the power-to-weight ratio of this versatile appliance. Now you can get the maximum benefits of this cookbook and make it last a lifetime with excellent food and wonderful health. Let this book be a guide to your success and let this cookbook become an inspiration to give your family healthy food in a more convenient and creative way. Let your family prepare their meals in a more creative and tasty way in every aspect. Let the benefits of this cookbook make you more aware of and more open to food and a healthy lifestyle. The quality of life depends upon the quality of food you eat.

As you enjoy more and more delicious and healthy food coming out of the kitchen, start looking forward to a highly satisfying experience with your new air fryer toaster oven. Get motivated as you prepare for healthy and delicious food that makes taste so much better without the deep flavors and the sharp tastes of so-called 'healthy meals'.